In Our Village

In Our Village

Kambi ya Simba Through the Eyes of Its Youth

BY THE STUDENTS OF AWET SECONDARY SCHOOL, TANZANIA, EAST AFRICA

AND WHAT KIDS CAN DO

Edited by Barbara Cervone

NEXT GENERATION PRESS

Providence, Rhode Island

Printed in Hong Kong by South Sea International Press, Ltd.
Distributed by National Book Network, Lanham, Maryland

ISBN 0-9762706-7-6
CIP data available.

Book design by Sandra Delany.

Next Generation Press, a not-for-profit book publisher, brings forward the
voices and vision of adolescents on their own lives, learning, and work.
With a particular focus on youth without privilege, Next Generation Press
raises awareness of young people as a powerful force for social justice.

Next Generation Press, P.O. Box 603252, Providence, Rhode Island 02906 U.S.A.
www.nextgenerationpress.org

10 9 8 7 6 5 4 3 2 1

Contents

Preface

IN TANZANIA, CLOSE TO THE TOWERING MT. KILIMANJARO, the vast plains of the Serengeti, and the Great Rift Valley, lies a village called Kambi ya Simba. It is a rural village, with one road in and one road out. Its 5,000 residents, spread over 40 square kilometers, are farmers. Their fortunes rise and fall with the crops and the weather. By every measure they are poor, in a country that ranks among the poorest in the world. They know scarcity, which can make "enough" seem like plenty. In a world of digital technology and designer coffee, they illuminate the night with lanterns and drink from streams and pumps that often carry illness.

Poverty alone does not define Kambi ya Simba. As in so many small villages across the African continent, life here holds much richness and many stories. Yet a romantic view of village life misses the mark, as its young people show us in this book. The village life they document is at once ordinary and surprising, entrepreneurial and backward. Its dreams are both wide and narrow, its times both good and bad. I asked Romana, one of the students on our project's team, what she likes best about the village. "Here, you know everything by heart," she said.

Kambi ya Simba first entered my own heart through my son, Carl, who started an agro-forestry project there while in college and now runs a microfinance program for rural women in a handful of Tanzanian villages. At once, I imagined a connection with the work of What Kids Can Do, our nonprofit organization whose mission is to bring youth voices to the public stage. Since its start in 2001, WKCD has worked closely with teenagers around the United States, using a variety of media to publish their thoughts on community, family, school, society, and, increasingly, global understanding. *In Our Village,* created with a team of secondary school students in Kambi ya Simba, marks our international debut, as the first project WKCD has carried out with young people outside North America.

I first met the students and faculty of the Awet Secondary School when my family and I visited Kambi ya Simba in December 2004. Their generous spirit and curiosity about the world was as large as their school was spare. The school's headmaster hoped that when we returned to the United States, I might raise funds for the school. Instead, I proposed another trip, this time to write a book with his students documenting life in Kambi ya Simba through the eyes of its youth. His generous assent gave *In Our Village* its start.

For two weeks in August 2005, I came back and worked with a team of Kambi ya Simba students, gathering the photographs and stories presented here. Our core group included ten student collaborators sixteen to eighteen years old, their three young teachers, my teenage son Daniel, and myself. On our last day, forty or more students crowded the classroom where we were meeting and joined the final stages of our process.

We began our work together by taking stock of the village's assets, whether hard or soft, ample or constrained. The students generated a list of thirty or more, from land, livestock, and tractors to friendship, faith, and the wisdom of elders. We narrowed the list to twenty and the students wrote down everything they knew about each, creating a common pool of knowledge from which to draw. In three teams, we then fanned out to collect the photographs and interviews that fill these pages. We worked on weekends and after school until the sun gave way to kerosene lamps. Each expedition to take photographs entailed walking five miles or more, stopping along the way to review photos and notes.

None of these students had ever held a camera before this project. Within minutes, however, they mastered the three digital cameras I brought, and thereafter they were loath to put them down. They took over a thousand photographs during our two weeks of work, and, with only a few exceptions, the pictures here are theirs.

Creating the accompanying narrative was less straightforward. Instruction at Awet Secondary School is in English, but neither students nor teachers are practiced in class discussions that are not linked to the prescribed curriculum. Moreover, I spoke "American"; they spoke "British" (and, of course, their national language *Kiswahili*); and some of the villager residents we interviewed spoke only the local *Iraqw*. We worked hard to understand each other.

For that reason, I have rendered here a mix of voices, hoping to make the "we" in this narration as true as possible to its diverse contributors: students, teachers, the villagers we interviewed, and local "experts" who provided many of the facts and figures. I drew, as well, on essays written by all 350 students at Awet Secondary School as part of our project. I tried hard to keep my own voice from intruding, seeking always to shape one coherent text from the words of many.

As we finished, I asked students to reflect on their work on this project. This is what they told me: It stretched our imagination in so many ways. Before this, we had never seen a book with photographs. Few of us have journeyed beyond the town of Karatu, nineteen kilometers distant. Of the larger world, we know only what our teachers have told us, a small encyclopedia we carry in our heads, containing facts and words, a few pictures, and no sound. Lacking electricity and computers, we have not traveled the Internet or watched other media that would show us life elsewhere, true or false.

Also, on our parting, they told me this: It astounds us—and we remain unconvinced—that anyone outside our village would care about our stories and our challenges. In a sense that goes beyond this phrase, your interest means the world to us. To us, it means "the world."

Barbara Cervone
Providence, Rhode Island
U.S.A.

Greetings

I N OUR VILLAGE AND THROUGHOUT TANZANIA, we greet each other from early in the morning until late at night. It is the way we start a conversation. We shake hands as part of the ritual. This communicates solidarity. We use an African handshake, which has three parts. We start by clasping right hands and, without letting go, we slip our hand around the other person's thumb, then go back to the clasped hands.

Our greetings vary depending on the ages of the two people, expressing respect along with friendship. So when a younger or lesser status person greets an older or higher status person, they say *shikamoo* (I respectfully greet you) and the person responds *marahaba* (I am delighted). When two adults of roughly equal status greet, they say *habari*. If it is morning, they might say *habari ya asubuhi*; if it is evening, they would say *habari ya jioni*. When two young people meet, one might say *mambo* or *vipi* to which the other might reply, *poa* or *safi*.

We also ask each other for news. How is everything at home? (*Habari za nyumbani?*) How are the children doing? (*Watoto wazima?*) *Hawajambo* (They are fine) or *salama* (well) are typical responses. We end the exchange with two words you will hear everywhere, all the time, in Tanzania: *karibu*, which means welcome or you are welcome, and *asante*, which means thank you.

For us, greeting and shaking hands is like breathing.

Soil covers our feet

THE LAND IS OUR LIFE IN KAMBI YA SIMBA. Soil, fields, pastures, streams, gardens, woodlands, these are the natural resources we hold close. In Tanzania, two-thirds of the population lives off the land. In our village, it is 100 percent. We are agro-pastoralists. Soil clings to our skin and covers our feet.

We measure our wealth by the land we own. The village government gives every family at least an acre. There we live with chickens poking about, perhaps a pile of maize, a compost heap, and a bucket of water. The prosperous among us own more land, a few as many as 30 acres. Their large fields meet the horizon.

One acre or thirty, land is a fragile resource. Jacob Casmiri Dallan, who for 35 years oversaw land and agriculture in our village, tells some history.

It is like this. In the 1950s, the British government was keen on proper land planning. In villages like Kambi ya Simba, they proposed separating the land for grazing, cultivation, and forests. They recommended proper agricultural methods. With independence in 1961, these plans disappeared. Good or bad, they had no following.

So we proceeded without plans. We knew how to subsist, but not how to sustain.

We grazed our cattle freely, harming our pastures. We plowed up hill and down, giving away our topsoil to the next heavy rain. We stripped forests for firewood, without replanting. And we grew. In 1960, our village had 700 people. Today there are almost 5,000.

Year after year, we took the fertility of our land for granted. We must now return to the soil the strength it once gave. For us, globalization starts under our feet.

Time has not, however, changed the spacious views across the Rift Valley to the east of our village or the huge shimmer from Lake Manyara. The soft panorama of mountains to the north and west makes us feel blessed.

Rivers and rain

IF LAND IS OUR LIFE, WATER IS OUR LIFE'S BLOOD. Our rivers flow down from the Ngorongoro Highlands, six kilometers to the north. The largest we call the River Seay. Like the *simba* (lions) for which our village is named, it crouches in a ravine at one turn, stretches out in full sun at another, barely moving.

The river and the rain go together, and with them our fortunes. The right amount of rainfall, and the harvest is strong. Too much rain, and seeds wash away. Too little, and soil crumbles in our hands. Wet and dry, these are our *majira* (seasons). Short rains (*mvuli*) come in November, long ones (*masika*) in March and April. Rainfall averages 800 mm (30 inches), but it can vary as much as 50 percent year to year. The past three years have been uncommonly steady, though: It has rained little in our village. Everything seems smaller.

For washing and cooking, we fetch much of our water from pumps. If you are lucky, the nearest pump may be just up the hill. If you are unlucky, it could be a walk of eight kilometers. Children—girls more often than boys—help collect water for their families.

They carry half-gallon jugs when they are young, and a gallon or more as they grow stronger.

We must preserve the water we have, just as we do the fertility of our land. Pantaleo Victory Paresso teaches geography at our school. He sees the village's rivers and streams drying up, and he worries:

> We have not been wise guardians of the water we receive. We graze cattle by the river's edge. This destroys the vegetation that restrains flooding when rain falls heavy. We lack irrigation or a system for trapping and storing rain. In dry times, like now, we have no reserve.
>
> We watch our permanent streams become temporary and temporary streams disappear. If the climate does not change, we may one day forget where our streams once flowed.

Adversity teaches us. In village seminars, we discuss how to begin conserving water. We bring whatever we have to the task: a rain barrel, a hose, a gutter that directs rain from a roof into a pail. Last year we planted 20,000 tree seedlings to regenerate soil.

Each *masika*, our teacher reminds us, brings hope and a second chance.

Wheat, maize, and papayas

AGRICULTURE MAKES UP HALF of Tanzania's gross domestic product. Most of what we plant in Kambi ya Simba, though, we eat ourselves or feed to our animals. Roughly half the village land is arable. Three-quarters of that is cultivated. Wheat is the closest thing we have to a cash crop, but *mahindi* (maize) covers 50 percent of our fields. We also grow *mbazi* (pigeon peas), beans, barley, and millet; and we raise sunflowers for their oil.

We have two growing seasons, November to February and April to July, which follow a set routine. We "inter-crop," growing crops in pairs and in rotation. We plant maize and pigeon peas in one season, wheat and beans the next. On the road into our village in May, gold and red nasturtiums sometimes carpet a field.

For a farmer, how much a crop yields matters more than anything else. In the past thirty years, our village has watched its crop yields fall. In 1974, wheat yielded 12 to 14 metric tons per acre. Now it yields less than three tons. The yield from maize has dropped to one-third of its former level.

Jacob Dallan, our village agricultural expert, explains:

Many factors affect harvest. Rain is one—not just the amount, but also the time it falls, neither too late nor too early. Fertility is second. Tired soil needs compost and fertilizer. Third comes good planting habits, like rotating crops. Then, there is seed quality. Basic seeds, where one year's plant produces next year's seed, do not compare well with the new, improved seeds you can buy with enough money. But the improved seeds do not produce more like them, to use in the following year.

Several women in our village have received small loans from a local development organization, to grow vegetables and fruit for sale. They have turned acres of land into bounty. They show the power of irrigation, fertilizer, strong seeds, and caring hands. "I grow papayas, tomatoes, spinach, carrots, lettuce, onions, even coffee," Lusia Antony boasts. "My customers, they make a parade. They ask, 'What is fresh today?'"

Living with livestock

IN OUR VILLAGE, LIVESTOCK COUNTS as family. We include animals in our yearly census. Records show that in 2004 we had 1,923 sheep, 1,910 goats, 1,900 chickens, 1,855 cows, 229 donkeys, and 75 pigs. We use cattle for milk and labor, chickens mostly for eggs, and sheep and goats for their hide. We trade livestock at the *mnada* (monthly market) that passes through our village. We rarely use our livestock for meat, except when a special occasion calls for a feast. When a family owns just a few animals, one sick cow spells hardship. The cost of veterinary medicine can exceed a month's income.

Joseph Tarmo is the agricultural and livestock field officer for Kambi ya Simba. He knows better than anyone how land, water, agriculture, and livestock mix in our village. What he says may come as a surprise.

The issue with livestock is not what you think. We have too many cattle, not too few. When we use cattle for their labor and milk, that is fine. But when we keep them for their value as property, maybe as a bride price, maybe to sell in times of trouble, this creates problems. It is a tradition across East Africa that makes us poorer, not richer.

Too many cattle stress the land, the water, the crops. When cattle graze freely, they also share diseases more easily. They produce poor breeds. "Fewer livestock. Zero grazing." In village seminars, this is what I teach. I see progress, but it is slow. You cannot tell a farmer in one day how to change a lifetime of habits.

One homestead, just north of the village center, puts "zero grazing" on display. In front of the house are five trees, with a pile of hay and an animal tied to each, so it may not graze freely. Each of them—two cows, a goat, a sheep, and a donkey—has a purpose, the old man, Anthoni, who owns them explains. "My wife, when she was younger, she carried the water. Now the donkey does."

If you think roosters crow only at dawn, you surely do not live with one. They sing *kokoreka* whenever they please.

Ugali

NOON AND NIGHT THE STIFF PORRIDGE *ugali* warms our stomachs. We make it from our maize, drying its kernels in the sun and then grinding them into flour. Once a week, rice and beans or chicken may change place with *ugali*. When we can, we eat spinach, carrots, potatoes, and other greens from local gardens. The sweet bananas from our trees are the length of an adult's middle finger. They sell for as little as 20 shillings (two cents) in the village center.

We wake in the morning to *chai* (tea) with milk, sometimes accompanied by *chapati*, a fried bread resembling a pancake and made with wheat flour. The restaurant, up a short hill from the village center, serves two dishes for dinner: rice and beans, and *chips-mayai*, a scrambled egg cooked with French fries. At school, we line up for our meals with a metal bowl in hand, scooping *ugali* from big pots into our dish.

Mama Elena, a primary school teacher who rents a room in the village center, describes the routine for cooking *ugali*:

First prepare the fire, from charcoal or small woods. Put a pan with water over the fire and allow it to boil, slightly. Start adding maize flour, stirring gently, gently with a *mwiko*. Add more flour, still stirring, gently, gently. Stir until it gets solid but not hard. When it is ready, the *ugali* separates from the sides of the pan. A sweet smell should touch your nose.

In times of scarcity we ration our food, sometimes eating just one meal a day. We share with those who have nothing. At weddings and funerals, especially after a harvest, everyone contributes to the table. Boiled sweet potatoes fill one bowl, rice and goat meat another.

In Tanzanian villages like ours, the average adult's daily caloric intake is estimated to be 1,900. The Food and Agriculture Organization of the United Nations recommends an adult daily minimum of 2,400 calories.

Two meters by three

SEVEN HUNDRED FAMILIES LIVE IN OUR VILLAGE. Homesteads stand next to fields and footpaths and dot hillsides and valleys throughout the 40 square kilometers of Kambi ya Simba. Our land is wide, but our homes are small. They may be just one room, two meters by three. You will not find a house with four rooms here.

We build our homes in several ways, depending on what we can afford. Houses with burnt brick walls and a corrugated iron roof are best. They last forever. But they are rare in our village. You must buy the iron roof and bricks in Karatu and then find a way to haul them up and down the hills to Kambi ya Simba. Houses with walls made from trees and soil or clay, topped with an iron roof, are next best. The wood adds sturdiness, but it is a precious resource. Most common are houses with grass roofs and walls made of dirt or cow dung. Both need refreshing every couple of years, though soil cakes more quickly than dung.

Volcus Clavery Mkamba, a student at Awet Secondary School, explains more:

Most homes in our village consist of two or three small rooms shared by six family members, usually two parents and four children. The rooms are in a line, with a sitting room in the middle and a door at the center. The sleeping rooms are on either side. Most often, the males sleep in one, the females in the other. At night, the livestock joins the family and the sitting room becomes theirs.

Sometimes a family will hang newspaper as decoration on the inside walls of the sitting room. It shows they are prosperous. When a daughter or son marries and moves to a house of their own, their families write good wishes in white paint on the outside walls, for everyone to see. If it is a son, they say *bahati nzuri* (good luck). If it is a daughter, they write *kwa heri* (farewell). They draw flowers to show their love.

After a strong harvest, we may use the extra income to expand our homestead. We might build an outhouse in the back or a small room for cooking by the side of the house.

The village dispensary

UNDER THE SHADOW OF HIV/AIDS, the average life expectancy in Tanzania has dropped to 44.5 years, by a 2005 estimate. In our village it is higher, close to 54 years. The same rough road that slows travel to and from our village also helps keep HIV/AIDS at a distance. Still, poverty and disease hold hands in our village, as they do across our country and all of Africa.

We practice vigilance as best we can. Yet bacteria infect the water we drink. Water-borne illness strikes a family member every three months on average, a recent village health survey found. When we cook inside, smoke from the burning coal or firewood fills our lungs. Malaria, which strikes all of us at least once, can turn chronic. Hepatitis, Rift Valley fever, typhoid—we know all their names.

We take simple illnesses to the village dispensary. For anything more, we find transport to the Lutheran Hospital in Karatu, if we can. We put on our best clothes, to show and receive respect from the doctors there.

Tanzania has only one doctor for every 50,000 persons. They are far outnumbered by traditional healers, and our village has two of these. If you visit Charles Mattay, you might find a large pot sitting on hot coals, bubbling away. Look inside and you will see vegetation, roots, and bark forming a dark liquid. A pungent smell fills the room.

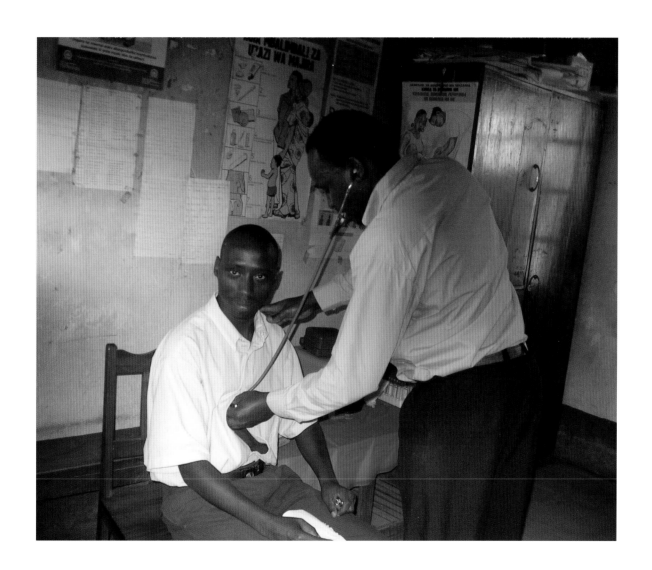

Most of us put our faith in modern medicine, though. We count on the aspirin and cough syrup sold at the village's small *duka la dawa* (drugstore) when we have a fever or a sore chest.

Amaniel Msemo has been the village doctor for ten years, working from a two-room dispensary three kilometers from the village center:

> Lower respiratory infections, diarrhea, malaria, intestinal worms, these are the diseases I treat most. Antibiotics are my weapons and I never have enough. Poor, overcrowded housing means that one family member's illness quickly becomes everyone's. Education helps. I hold workshops for the village. I dispense health education as much as I give out medicines and listen to hearts. As for poverty, I have no cure.

Twenty customers a day

SOME OF US YEARN TO BE ENTREPRENEURS. In a country so recently socialist, this may seem strange. But we welcome commerce, however modest.

Our stores come in three sizes. *Dukas* are the largest, made of sturdy walls and a roof, with goods stacked on shelves and maybe a brass scale for weighing rice. *Kiosks*, smaller wooden shacks, have fewer items for sale. *Bandas* are the smallest, narrow stands made with sticks that sell fruits and vegetables.

A small concentration of stores, perhaps a dozen in all, lines the dirt strip in the village center. Most stock basic household goods. A few specialize, like the drugstore for animals. Outside the center, *dukas* and *kiosks* appear wherever homesteads collect. Each carries a few staples, like sugar, kerosene, and hard candies. At the north end of the village, there is a *kiosk* whose keeper sells dried anchovies and potatoes.

For the many things that we cannot buy from each other, we use the traveling market that passes each month. We look and barter, maybe for a new aluminum pot or a pair of manufactured trousers.

Kornelia Damiano and her husband are among our village's entrepreneurs. Above the cooking oil and toothpaste in their small store, a sign reads, "*Kukopesha ni kupoteza wateja*" ("To loan is to lose clients"). Kornelia says:

> We know our customers' needs. We sell a little of a lot. Sugar, soap, magazines, soda, candles, notebooks, vegetable oil, flashlights, pens, toothpaste, biscuits, batteries, tea, matches—flip-flops, too. We open at seven in the morning and close at nine at night, when a kerosene lantern lights our shelves. We receive twenty customers a day—enough, but we wish for more. Sometimes people do not buy, but just visit. They make company.

For customers who want to wrap their purchases instead of carrying them loose, Kornelia sells a page of newspaper for ten shillings (a penny).

Ox-plows and tractors

As long as anyone can remember, we have tilled the fields in our village with hand-hoes. Animal traction, in the form of ox-plows, is a more recent practice. Oxen reduce the drudgery, but they are worth the investment only if they make the land more productive. They pull a disc plow or weeder, and when these break, it takes a blacksmith to repair them. We do not have a blacksmith in Kambi ya Simba.

We like tractors very much, on the other hand. Ten farmers in our village own tractors at this time. They were fortunate enough either to secure a tractor loan from the Tanzanian government or to reap several large harvests in a row. The government also gives loans for tractor repairs. This shows foresight. It can cost as much money to maintain a tractor as to purchase one.

Filimini Bura Hayshi and his brother bought a Massey-Ferguson tractor in 1995 for 2.5 million shillings (roughly $4,000 USD in '95). They have turned it into a business:

We charge to plow fields and carry loads, to transport supplies from nearby villages or wood to build houses. Last year, we charged 12,000 shillings ($12 USD) to plow an acre. Customers come to us; we never have to advertise. This year, with the price of oil higher, I think we will have to raise our price. Still, everyone benefits from our tractors. That is what people say.

Even when aided by animals or tractors, plowing, weeding, and harvesting are hard work. Some people in our village say the labor keeps them young. Others say it makes them old.

A bumpy ride

IN OUR VILLAGE, OUR FEET CARRY US EVERYWHERE. Kilometers and kilometers of dirt paths criss-cross our land. The north end of our village stands at 1,800 meters (5,906 feet), the south at 1,300 meters (4,265 feet). More small valleys than you can count lie between those two points. Walking means going up one hill and down another. Everything slopes, including our fields. We know our footpaths by heart. At night, especially at the full moon, we find our way by a bend in the path, a silhouette of trees, a maize field.

Bicycles also provide transportation, for those who can afford one. They are a prized possession. There may be as many as 100 bicycles in our village; it is difficult to keep track. You will see few females riding bicycles, but we suspect that will soon change.

Wilfred Maho, a farmer and bicycle owner, says:

I dreamed of owning a bike for several years. Last year my crops made me lucky and I saved the money I needed. I searched the streets and shops of Karatu for the right bike, not brand new, not old, one as strong as me. The bicycle I found may not be perfect, but it makes me happy. When I can, I give other people a ride. The rider sits crossways on the bar in front of the seat, getting off to walk if we come to a hill. I will tell you this: If you ride a bike in Kambi ya Simba, you must know how to patch a tire.

Transportation out of Kambi ya Simba takes patience. Ruts and stones cover the dirt road that connects our village to Karatu, nineteen kilometers away.

A *dala dala* (public bus) makes two trips a day. Passengers of all sizes, vegetables, boxes of supplies, sometimes live chickens—they form a big jumble, one on top of another. The overflow, including humans, joins the luggage on the roof. Most times the trip takes an hour, longer when the bus breaks down.

In 1996, Tanzania had an average of one motor vehicle for every 1,000 inhabitants. The number has increased a lot since then, but it is still low by most counts. Our village of 5,000 has eight vehicles, all of them with four-wheel drive. We have five motorcycles, too. In March and April, the rain makes the dirt road between Kambi ya Simba and Karatu impassable except by foot. Our shoes sink deep into its mud.

Wireless

ELECTRICITY REACHES LESS THAN 10 PERCENT of Tanzania's population. In rural areas, that drops to almost zero. In our village, four small generators provide all the electricity we have. We run them until they die. They lead short lives.

Yet almost 20 percent of our villagers now own mobile phones (*simu*). Farmers with crops or livestock to sell in markets outside Kambi ya Simba call ahead and find where they will obtain the best price. "It puts me in front," one farmer says. Our teachers use their mobiles to communicate with each other, with families and friends living elsewhere, and with the world beyond.

In 2003, about 6 percent of Tanzanians had access to a telephone, and 70 percent of these used cellular phones.

Lazaro Xumay Gidri has found a way to link a generator to digital technology and make money:

I bought a generator in Arusha for 250,000 shillings ($250 USD), along with a satellite antenna, television, VCR, and two fluorescent lights. I set everything up in a room in the center. For 300 shillings (30 cents) people can charge their mobile phones. At eight in the evening, people come to watch the news on satellite TV. They pay 100 shillings (10 cents) for ten minutes of news.

With the VCR, I show American action movies and movies from Nigeria. I charge for that, too. For football games, the cost depends on the stakes, from 200 to 300 shillings per game. Fuel for the generator costs me 2,000 shillings ($2) a day.

In much of our country, the world of electricity and digital technology still seems far away. Firewood accounts for 92 percent of the nation's total energy consumption. Kerosene lamps provide the light for our village.

Solar energy, we are learning, may one day meet our needs. We just acquired a small solar battery, which powers one light bulb in an office in the village center.

Made by hand

MOST PEOPLE in our village just want enough. The market for fancy goods does not exist. We have three carpenters, each with an apprentice. That is plenty, because we do not have much furniture. A table, a few chairs and benches, a bed frame or two—our homes do not have space for more than this.

We have rope makers, too, and they do a steady business. They weave sisal and fiber from leaves into thick coils. We use rope to tie livestock to trees or to tether animals as they graze. A good rope for livestock lasts six months. The rope we use for tying firewood lasts a year.

Making clothes on foot-powered sewing machines gives the most opportunity for business here. In our village, twelve women do the sewing, stitching mostly female clothes. If you have seen our *kangas*, the cotton cloth Tanzanian women wear for skirts and tops, you know how much bold patterns and bright colors mean to us. Even the pleated skirts of our school uniforms are bright orange.

In cities like Arusha, males dominate the sewing business. They set up shop on the sidewalks, making men's trousers and jackets in full view. They sell what they make in open-air markets, competing with vendors selling *mitumba* (used clothing).

Paskalina William has owned a sewing machine for two years. She sells dresses in a *duka* in the village center:

> To become a seamstress, I went to vocational school in Mbulu for a year. I buy fabric from special stores in Arusha, not from the street stalls that sell common cloth. I make clothes for girls and women. I sew everything from *sari za shule* (school uniforms) to wedding gowns. Some clients prefer a white gown, others prefer colored.
>
> I follow patterns that I keep in a notebook, but sometimes I create my own design, from pictures in my head. The money is good. When a dress I sew makes a woman feel special, that is good too.

Singing and dancing

IN JOY OR SORROW, WE AFRICANS SING AND DANCE. Our adult choir, *kwaya* in Swahili, performs as often as it can. "We sing for our hearts," one member says. They sing and dance with a purpose as well—to educate, uplift, inspire, and warn. One song they perform is called "*Historia ya Ukimwi*." It tells how HIV/AIDS came to Tanzania from two Ugandan businessmen, and how it affects our families and society.

Like the adults, we sing for our hearts too. This year, our school choir won first prize at the district choir competition. We beat 50 competitors, many from schools larger than ours.

As much as we like making music, we like listening. Day and night, music from battery-operated radios drifts from a house here or there or from a *duka* in the village center. The sounds of *Bongo Fleva* (Tanzanian hip-hop), *Juma Nature*, or religious hymns tell you who is controlling the radio dial. At school, we listen to the latest songs whenever we can. We dance a lot, and some of us rap.

John Elibariki, a student at our school, wants to be a musician. He enjoys hip-hop but also sings in the school choir:

> Our choir, *ukwata*, practices after school for several hours, five days a week. For the district competition, we prepared two songs. The first was the national anthem, "*Wimbo wa Taifa*," which we performed as a church hymn. The second, "*Sikieni Watu Wote*," is an educational song. It tells the dangers of AIDS, alcohol, and drugs. It begins with the word "*Sikieni!*" ("Listen!")

For musical instruments, the village keeps two guitars and twenty drums spread out among our three churches and school. Some people also play homemade drums.

The more you win, the more you play

YOU WILL NOT SEE TANZANIA'S FOOTBALL TEAM in the World Cup. You will not find our school's name on a silver trophy. Still, we cheer our school's football players as if they were champions. After school, one form (grade level) challenges another on a nearby field. It has no lines marked on it, so "out of bounds" is a matter of opinion. The best players get picked for the school team. They wear their yellow and green uniforms when they compete against other villages.

Girls play netball, a team game based on running, jumping, throwing, and catching. The rules say only fourteen players may take the court at one time, but we allow as many as want to play. The aim is to score as many goals as possible from within an area called the goal circle. On our court, the goal circle markings are imaginary.

Two board games are popular in our village. *Bao* involves distributing, capturing, and redistributing sixty-four seeds on a game board with four rows of eight holes. It belongs to the *mancala* game family. *Mancala* is one of the oldest board games in the world, although no one knows how old. It may have begun as a game played in holes scooped in the sand or earth. Many people say *bao* tests the limits of the human mind.

Drafti, or draughts, is also an old game, left behind by the British. It is checkers, with a little chess. Men play it in the village center, using bottle caps for pieces. You win the game if you take all of your opponent's pieces, if they cannot make any more moves, or if they give up.

Emanuel Bayo has played *drafti* for just one year. He already claims the village title, and no one argues with that.

I play after I finish my work, as often as I can. I study my mistakes and do not make them again. That is my champion's secret. The people I play, most have been playing for eight or nine years.

In *drafti* you keep playing until you lose, one opponent after another. The more you win, the more you play. I get to play a lot.

Good friends

THEY SAY TANZANIANS ARE THE FRIENDLIEST people on earth. We would not know. We can tell you this, though: When two people pass each other on our footpaths, they say hello. We greet and shake hands all the time, eager to exchange news. We care about unity. We treat strangers as friends. We show respect and good behavior in the language we use. When someone enters a room or we want their attention, we say *karibu sana* (most welcome) several times. When we need something, we say not only *tafadhali* (please) but also *naomba* (I beg of you).

And we smile.

Since few people leave our village, friendships last a lifetime. We make friends at the places you would expect: church, school, special events, and celebrations. Our nearest neighbor may live a ten-minute walk away, but we call on each other for company and help. Disputes are rare and they never last long. We do not snatch from one another. We share. Only once in ten years has a case of stealing in our village needed to go to the court in Karatu. We do not have a court here.

When you are our age, what makes someone a good friend?

A good friend is someone you can exchange ideas with. — TRIPHONIA

A good friend helps you with your subjects. — HEAVENLIGHT

A friend is someone who values you. — SYLVESTER

Heavenlight is my best friend. She has good behavior. She keeps secrets.
We talk about science studies together, and we laugh, too. — SHANGWE

The walk from one point to another in our village can be long. It strengthens friendships along with muscles, one of our teachers says. We share stories that go on for kilometers.

Village government

JIANDAE KUHESABIWA." ("Prepare to be counted.") The fliers say that, announcing each year's village census. Perhaps because we have so few hard assets, we count

all the ones we have. The village government compiles the record. In 2004, the inventory—maybe 30 items long—included 2,583 males and 2,347 females, 54 ox-carts, 225 dogs, and 6 grinding machines.

Village government also handles official decisions and rules. Sometimes the matter is strictly local, and we talk it out until we agree. Other times, the decisions come from far away. The village government oversees social services, too—education, water, animal husbandry, and the medical dispensary. It administers the warehouse where farmers store crops, seeds and fertilizer, and machinery needing repair. It even tames our bees. In the one-room government office, you will see a beekeeper's suit in a corner.

We elect an executive director and 25 councilors every five years. Anyone eighteen and older can vote, and by law, ten percent of the councilors must be women. Laurenti

Crescenti, our village executive director, is also a farmer. Few of his duties require him to sit behind a desk, so the doors to his office are often closed. He explains his job:

I monitor the village decisions and execute orders from the district and beyond. I secure the peace. When there is a dispute, perhaps over property held in common, people turn to me.

Three times a year, the village councilors and I hold a village assembly where people ask questions and speak complaints. We talk of our needs, too. If we are to bring more teachers to our primary school, we must build them houses. To bring more tractors to our fields, we must petition the district government. We discuss and make plans, many plans.

To questions like "Why is the dispensary always low on supplies?" or "Why do we not have better access to improved seed varieties?" there are often few answers, or really, just one: We lack money.

Writing down every word

WE ARE HUNGRY FOR EDUCATION HERE, as much as we can get. In our village, we have a nursery, two primary schools, and a secondary school. A half-hour's walk separates each from the other. The secondary school is new, but thirty years of chalk-dust whiten the primary school blackboards. The primary school has over 850 students in eight grades, and 60 to 75 pupils to a class. Three hundred and fifty students attend secondary, which has four forms and 40 to 50 pupils per class.

We sit at wooden desks lined up in rows. The breeze blows through our classrooms. The walls are bare. We wear uniforms and when called on we always stand, prefacing our remarks with "Sir" and "Madam." In secondary school, we take ten subjects, and speak only English. Our teachers are young and, we believe, wise.

In Tanzania, only one in ten primary students achieve secondary school. Primary school is free, but secondary carries a tuition. In our village it costs 20,000 shillings ($20 USD) a year, and parents must also donate, per term, 36 kilograms of maize and

13 kilograms of beans for day students, or 95 kilograms of maize and 34 kilograms of beans for hostel dwellers. We advance from form to form depending on how we score on national exams. If you are weak in a subject, help is scarce. One-quarter of our country's population cannot read and write.

Herieli Malle, the headmaster of Awet Secondary School, believes education holds the key to our village's future:

In the past, many did not see the validity of a thorough education. In a village of agro-pastoralists, a primary education seemed plenty. Now we know our children need the most education we can give, including our girls.

Families sacrifice all they can to pay the school fees. We lack textbooks and so much more. Our teachers fill their blackboards with knowledge, and our students write down every word.

Our students care about the affairs of the world. Some topics, they are abstractions. Others, like global warming, affect them directly. They wonder if the drought in our village may become permanent. They wonder why the industrialized world does not do more to control dangerous emissions. The global community, our students want to be contributing members. They are fierce in their studies and in their will to belong.

God's blessings

CHURCH BRINGS PEOPLE TOGETHER in our village, and we have three: a Catholic, a Lutheran, and a Pentecostal church. Some of us attend churches in nearby villages, like the Roman Catholic Church in Upper Kitete, 12 kilometers away.

In Tanzania, there are equal numbers of Christians, Muslims, and followers of native religions, and we value religious tolerance. In Kambi ya Simba, we are mostly Christians, yet we welcome all faiths.

We go to church on Sundays to support each other—and to pray. Praying together is always more effective than praying alone, we believe, and we pray a lot: for rain, recovery from sickness, a good harvest, a safe journey, stronger cattle. We seek God's blessing for special occasions, too, from weddings, births and deaths to a football competition with a nearby village.

In a village with few books, the Bible is the first text we hold in our hands. Reading the verses helps us relate to the transformations in our own lives.

But it is the music that often lures us most to church. Every church has a *kwaya* (choir), and singing, dancing, drumming, and folk tales spill out the door. Audio cassettes (*kandas*) of church music have become a big business across Tanzania.

Robert Masong, the minister at our village's Lutheran church, reports:

> The church was built in 1994, at which time its members were using a classroom for their prayers. The new church enabled nearly 300 members of the community to attend. Five people regularly work for the church—a caretaker, an evangelist, and several others part-time.

> Each Sunday, the caretaker and evangelist commence the service. The service has a choir as a way of attracting anyone at all to pray with us. In addition to worship, the church is blessed with a one and a half acre farm to support itself. The church we built ten years ago is already worn out and unsatisfactory. We have put in place a plan to build a new one.

As for providing charity, our churches step in when they can. They may help one family with school fees and another with medicine for a sick child.

Children and sacrifice

CHILDREN FILL OUR VILLAGE. Forty-four percent of the population in Tanzania is under fourteen. We are a young country, though this may be changing. Fifteen years ago, the average mother in Kambi ya Simba gave birth to six live babies. Now our average birth rate has dropped to 3.8.

Once it was good to have a lot of children. They fetched water and firewood; they herded cattle and goats; they gathered vegetables; they went to the store. They did whatever their parents needed. They stood in for wealth. Now, having too many children can extend poverty. Children need development; they need education. And this *takes* wealth.

Angela Marco Malle, a mother of four, says:

When I was a child, work, not school, made my life. That is the way it was, especially if you were a girl. Parents saw their children as fruit for the labor they provided, and they picked them early. Now, children are our fruit for the future they bring, not the water they carry. And rather than pick them early, we must let them ripen.

In my household, I am the father and the mother. I do the work of two. I want my three sons and daughter to have the education that I never had. Yes, I want my children to help me when I am old. Yes, I want them to have good manners. But I also want them to find what they are good at, to acquire the education that makes them strong. I tell them they must do real work and control their lives.

As young people, we are grateful for the sacrifices of our families. We want to give back.

I want to help street children by giving them food, clothes, and shelter. — LUCY JOSEPH

I want to ensure that the women in my country get the education they deserve and the right to inherit land. — LUCY JOSEPH

I want to deliver my country from poverty and disease. — JULIUS

I would like to balance the budget of the country. — PIUS

I want to teach people about good agricultural and industrial practices that will help our country develop. — WAYDAELI

I want to help protect the environment, especially the ozone layer, so that we preserve our planet. — PILI

I would like to use knowledge effectively in order to fight oppression of any kind. — PASCHALINA

They call me Yame

WHEN GREETING SOMEONE OLDER THAN YOU in Swahili, you say *"shikamoo"* to show respect. Only 2.5 percent of Tanzania's population is over 65. In our village, that includes about 140 people. Our elders form a village council. They meet to share memories and discuss village affairs. We consider their knowledge sacred.

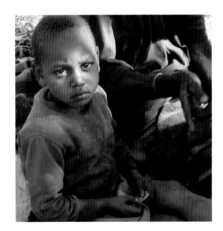

Elders in our village never live alone. Generations sleep under the same roof and eat from the same pot. We give each other strength.

The oldest person in Kambi ya Simba is 103 years old.

My name is Emanuel. They call me Yame. I was born in 1902, in the village of Mbulu. School ended for me after one year. The head teacher asked my parents if I would care for his cattle. My parents said yes.

I fought in World War II. Carrying a gun to shoot people, that made me unhappy. It went against my nature. I have yet to be paid for my service in World War II. I still ask the government, Where is my money? They never answer. After the war, I was appointed Minister of Peace and Safety for the Mbulu-Karatu district. It was a job that made me proud.

I have outlived my wives. My first wife, she died after our second child was born. That was before I went to fight in the war. My second wife, she died last year. I have eight children. My great-grandchildren, they keep me company, here in the sun.

When I first came to the village, we had to chase away the lions. That is why it is called *Kambi ya Simba* (Lion's Camp). We killed elephants when they threatened us, and ate their meat.

For many years, I staged traditional plays and dances for the village. I was the village healer, too. Medicinal roots, I know what they cure and how to apply them.

Some days I worry for our village. The rains are fewer. The soil is poorer. But we are a strong people. We care for each other. When I sit here, outside on my blanket, everyone who passes says *"shikamoo."*

I want to be a leader

F EW STUDENTS WHO GRADUATE FROM OUR SCHOOL continue their studies. The reason is simple: we cannot afford university tuition. In our daily lives, we make do with so little. It breaks our hearts that we must do without further education, too. Still, we dream of our future—dreams that would take us away from the village we know so well:

I want to be a scientist in order to reach the sky as American scientists have. — FAUSTINE

I want to be a journalist or a reporter and travel to Europe. — REBEKA

I want to be the headmistress at a secondary school. — GOODNESS

I want to be president of Tanzania. — LUCY

I want to be a pilot. — SHANGWE

I want to have only four children, if God wishes, by use of family planning. — MATLE

I want to be a doctor in a modern hospital. — PASCALINA

I want to be a teacher at the university. — EMELIANA

I want to be a pastor in my church. — RUBEN

I dream to continue my studies in another country. God bless me for my opinion. — CLAUDIA

I want to be a tour guide in a national park. — HEAVENLIGHT

I want to be an artist. I also want to work in a radio station. — HALIMA

I would like to be an agricultural officer. — VICTORY

I imagine being a secretary in an office. — ROZINA

I would like to open my own school and I will name it Tenga Academic School. — FUMENCE

I want to be a doctor and a musician. I want to run my life softly. — GLORY

I want to be a teacher of Kiswahili. — PILI

I want to be a lawyer. — FISSOO

I want to be a driver of big cars. — MODEST

I want to be a master of literature. — REGINALD

I would like to be a peaceful person. — LUCIAN

I want to be a leader in my country. — THOBIAS

More about Tanzania

TANZANIA LIES IN EAST AFRICA, just south of the equator. It is home to many of the postcard images of Africa: Mount Kilimanjaro (the tallest mountain in Africa, at 19,340 feet), the Serengeti Plains (where wild animals roam one of the oldest ecosystems on earth), Ngorongoro (a 10,000 foot volcano whose collapsed caldera is 10 miles in diameter and which boasts the world's densest population of predators), the red-clad Maasai herdsmen, the Great Rift Valley (a 6,000 mile crack in the earth's crust), the island of Zanzibar (known for its spices), and Lake Victoria (the largest lake in Africa and the source of the Nile).

Within Tanzania's borders one finds the Olduvai Gorge (the "Cradle of Life" where the Leakeys unearthed the oldest hominid fossils), Gombe Stream (where Jane Goodall does her chimpanzee research), and the town of Ujiji (where the explorer Henry M. Stanley said the famous words, "Doctor Livingstone, I presume?"). There is Lake Tanganyika (the second deepest lake in the world), the Selous Game Reserve (the largest protected reserve in Africa, covering an area greater than that of Switzerland) and Oldonyo Lengai (the world's only active carbonate volcano, whose lavas can be approached at close range and look like melted chocolate).

Tanzania also has miles of white sand beaches, savannahs, tropical rainforests, petrified deserts, verdant hills, and some of the world's finest coral reefs. It has the second richest bird catalogue and the largest animal migration—over one million Serengeti wildebeests—in the world.

Culturally, the population is hugely diverse, with over 120 indigenous cultures. Tanzania is the only country in Africa whose people speak four of the continent's five linguistic families: Bantu (the most common family in Africa), Cushitic (with roots in Mesopotamia, hence the name of its speakers, the Iraqw), Nilotic (coming from Nubian populations in the Nile Valley), and Khoisan (with click-sounds, the language of "Bushmen"). Unlike most of Tanzania's neighbors, where such diversity has been the catalyst for civil war, Tanzania has a peaceful history. A single language, Swahili, unites its many groups.

In terms of religion, Tanzania splits in thirds. Christian, Muslim, and traditional faiths claim a roughly equal number of followers. People on the coast and the island of Zanzibar are mostly Muslim. Inland, they are more often Christians. The animists are found usually in remote, rural areas.

Tanganyika was a German colony until the end of World War I, when it came under British rule. It gained independence in 1961, and then merged with Zanzibar to form Tanzania in 1964. Julius Nyerere became president and, soon after, turned the country towards socialism. Nyerere was a charismatic leader, and though his socialist policies were catastrophic for the country's economy, his reign was peaceful and he is still regarded as the "father of Tanzania."

In 1986, after Nyerere's resignation opened the way to democratic elections, the country embarked on reforms designed to strengthen the economy and encourage foreign investment. Since then, Tanzania has made positive strides, both socially and economically. The international community has offered encouragement, with Europe, the United States, and the international lending institutions agreeing to help reduce the country's roughly seven billion dollars of debt.

Still, Tanzania remains one of the least developed countries in the world. Per capita gross domestic product (GDP) equaled $520 (USD) in 2004, making it the second poorest country in the world (with a measurable GDP), next to Sierra Leone. Agriculture makes up half of the country's GDP. Tourism and mining are the country's fastest growing sectors, but they are controlled largely by non-blacks. Most Tanzanians are subsistence farmers in rural districts, served by bad roads and living without electricity, running water, or basic sanitation. Minimum wage is set at $50 per month in urban areas and $35 per month in rural areas, though informal employers often pay a fraction of this. Nearly half the country lives below the national poverty line of $180 per year.

Life expectancy in Tanzania has dropped from 49.5 years in 1975 to 46.0 years in 2005. While AIDS/HIV rates in Tanzania are relatively low by African standards—recent estimates suggest an infection rate of 8 percent—they have still taken a toll. The childhood mortality rate stands at 16.5 percent, with malaria and water-borne illnesses the leading killers. Almost half of Tanzania's children are undernourished, and the average woman gives birth to five children.

Enrollment in primary schools has increased steadily in recent years, the result of the Tanzanian government's decision to make primary education universal and free. However, facilities are threadbare, and most teachers are insufficiently trained. The student teacher ratio can range from as high as 222:1 in some rural schools to 66:1 in urban areas. Secondary school enrollments have also increased. Secondary education is not free, though, and tuition fees, paired with rigorous admission exams, put it beyond the reach of most. Only one in ten primary students advances to secondary school. Post-secondary education remains a brass ring that few catch. In 2000, the total university enrollment for Tanzania was 20,000 students.

Breathtakingly beautiful, diverse, and poor, Tanzania tests resilience and hope every day.

(From "A Tanzanian Backgrounder," by Carl Cervone, June 2005)

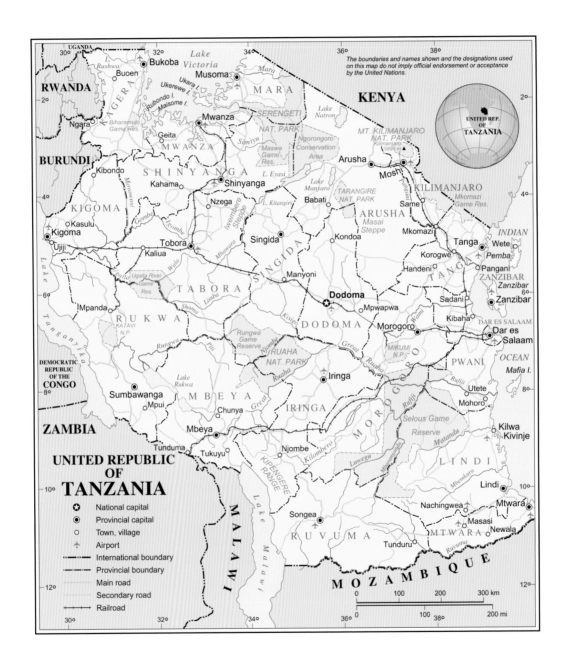

The boundaries and names shown and the designations used on this map do not imply official endorsement or acceptance by the United Nations.

UNITED REP. OF TANZANIA

RWANDA

BURUNDI

DEMOCRATIC REPUBLIC OF THE CONGO

ZAMBIA

UNITED REPUBLIC OF TANZANIA

⊛ National capital
◉ Provincial capital
○ Town, village
✈ Airport
—··— International boundary
—·—· Provincial boundary
——— Main road
——— Secondary road
+—+—+ Railroad

UGANDA

Lake Victoria

KENYA

MARA

SERENGETI NAT. PARK

Lake Natron

MT. KILIMANJARO NAT. PARK
Kilimanjaro 5895 m ▲

Maswe Game Res.

Ngorongoro Conservation Area

MWANZA

SHINYANGA

L. Eyasi

Lake Manyara

TARANGIRE NAT. PARK

KILIMANJARO

ARUSHA

Masai Steppe

Mkomazi Game Res.

INDIAN

KIGOMA

SINGIDA

TABORA

DODOMA

RUKWA

KATAVI N.P.

Rungwa Game Reserve

RUAHA NAT. PARK

MIKUMI N.P.

PWANI

ZANZIBAR

DAR ES SALAAM

OCEAN

Mafia I.

MBEYA

IRINGA

MOROGORO

Selous Game Reserve

LINDI

ZAMBIA

KIPENGERE RANGE

RUVUMA

MTWARA

MALAWI

Lake Malawi

MOZAMBIQUE

Bukoba
Buoen
Musoma
Ngara
Mwanza
Geita
Ukerewe I.
Ukara I.
Rubondo I.
Maisome I.
Biharamulo Game Res.
Kibondo
Kahama
Shinyanga
Nzega
Kasulu
Kigoma
Ujiji
Tobora
Kaliua
Singida
Babati
Arusha
Moshi
Same
Mkomazi
Tanga
Wete
Pemba
Korogwe
Handeni
Pangani
Zanzibar
Kondoa
Manyoni
Dodoma
Mpwapwa
Morogoro
Sadani
Kibaha
Dar es Salaam
Mpanda
Sumbawanga
Mpui
Chunya
Mbeya
Tunduma
Tukuyu
Njombe
Iringa
Utete
Mohoro
Kilwa Kivinje
Lindi
Songea
Tunduru
Nachingwea
Masasi
Newala
Mtwara

Lake Rukwa
Lake Tanganyika

0   100   200   300 km
0   100   200 mi

Other facts

LOCATION: East Africa, bordering the Indian Ocean, between Kenya and Mozambique

AREA: 945,087 square kilometers

ARABLE LAND: 4.52% (2003)

IRRIGATED LAND: 0.16% (1998)

CLIMATE: Varies from tropical along the coast to temperate in highlands

TOTAL POPULATION: 36.7 million (2005)

AGE: 0–14 years, 44%; 15–64 years, 53.4%; 65 years and over, 2.6 % (2005)

URBAN POPULATION (% of total): 35.4% (2003)

POPULATION GROWTH RATE: 1.83% (2005)

LITERACY: 78.2%: male, 85.9% and female, 70.7% (2003)

GOVERNMENT TYPE: Republic

CAPITAL: Dodoma

INDEPENDENCE: Tanganyika became independent on December 9, 1961 (from a United Kingdom–administered United Nations trusteeship). Zanzibar became independent on December 9, 1963 (from the United Kingdom). Tanganyika united with Zanzibar on April 26, 1964 to form the United Republic of Tanganyika and Zanzibar; it was renamed the United Republic of Tanzania on October 29, 1964.

AGRICULTURAL PRODUCTS: Coffee, sisal (used to make rope), tea, cotton, pyrethrum (insecticide made from chrysanthemums), cashew nuts, tobacco, cloves, corn, wheat, cassava (manioc), bananas, fruits, vegetables, cattle, sheep, goats

INDUSTRIAL PRODUCTS: Agricultural processing (sugar, beer, cigarettes, sisal twine), gemstones, gold and iron mining, soda ash, oil refining, shoes, cement, apparel, wood products, fertilizer, salt

PUBLIC EXPENDITURE ON EDUCATION (% of GDP): 2.9% (2002)

PUBLIC EXPENDITURE ON HEALTH (% of GDP): 2.7% (2002)

POPULATION WITH SUSTAINABLE ACCESS TO IMPROVED SANITATION: 46% (2002)

INTERNET USERS (per 1,000 people): 7 (2002)

(Statistics from *Human Development Report* 2005, United Nations Development Program)

Swahili glossary

(Assembled by students and teachers at Awet Secondary School)

Greetings

hello/how are you? *habari*

I'm fine (reply back) *nzuri*

greetings (to an elder) *shikamoo*

reply (to an elder) *marahaba*

greetings (youth-to-youth) *mambo* or *vipi*

reply (youth-to-youth) *poa* or *safi*

may I come in? *hodi*

welcome/come in *karibu*

good morning *habari ya asubuhi*

goodbye *kwa heri*

good luck *bahati*

Other civilities

please *tafadhali*

thank you *asante*

thank you very much *asante sana*

you're welcome *karibu*

you're very welcome *karibu sana*

forgive me *samahani*

sorry *pole*

I beg of you *naomba*

Inquiries (*habari + noun*)

how is your work? *habari za kazi?*

how is everything at home? *habari za nyumbani*

how are your studies? *habari za masomo?*

how are you this morning *habari ya asubuhi*

how are you this evening? *habari za jioni*

possible reply: "fine" *salama*

Forms of address

Bibi is a term of respect used to address women. *Mama* is a term of great respect and is usually used to address older women. *Bwana* is a term of respect for men, meaning "sir" or "mister." *Mzee* means "elder" or "old person." *Rafiki* means "friend."

Some basics

yes *ndiyo*

no *hapana*

maybe *labda*

easy *rahisi*

hard *ngumu*

okay *sawa/haya*

and *na*

or *au*

but *lakini*

big *kubwa*

little *ndogo* or *kidogo*

good *nzuri*

bad *mbaya*

today *leo*

tomorrow *kesho*

yesterday *jana*

Numbers

one *moja*

two *mbili*

three *tatu*

four *nne*

five *tano*

six *sita*

seven *saba*

eight *nane*

nine *tisa*

ten *kumi*

twenty *ishirini*

fifty *hamsini*

hundred *mia*

thousand *elfu*

million *milioni*

Colors

black *nyeusi*

white *nyeupe*

red *nyekundu*

blue *blu*

green *kijani*

yellow *njano*

khaki *kaki*

brown *rangi ya udongo*

orange *rangi ya machungwa*

SOME WORDS IN THIS BOOK

AIDS *ukimwi*

assistance *msaada*

audio cassette *kanda*

banana *ndizi*

beans *maharagwe*

bicycle *baisikeli*

bird/airplane *ndege*

book *kitabu*

boy *mvulana*

bucket *ndoo*

cat *paka*

cattle *ng'ombe*

chalkboard *ubao*

chicken *kuku*

children *watoto*

choir *kwaya*

church *kanisa*

clothes *nguo*

communication *mawasiliano*

cooking fire *moto wa kupikia*

cooking pot *chungu* or *sufuria*

day *siku*

daytime *mchana*

desk *dawati*

doctor *daktari* or *mganga*

dog *mbwa*

donkey *punda*

dream *ndoto*

dress *gauni*

drought *ukame*

drugstore *duka la dawa*

dust *uvumbi*

education *elimu*

electricity *umeme*

elephant *tembo* or *ndovu*

family *familia*

farmer *mkulima*

father *baba*

field *shamba*

flour *unga*

fried bread *chapati*

fruits *matunda*

game *mchezo*

girl *msichana*

goat *mbuzi*

hair *nywele*

health *afya*

hill *kilima*

homestead *makazi* or *nyumbani*

journey *safari*

kerosene *mafuta ya taa*

land *ardhi*

lantern *taa*

lion *simba*

livestock *mifugo*

maize *mahindi*

maize porridge *ugali*

meat *nyama*

medicine *dawa*

milk *maziwa*

mobile phone *simu*

money *fedha* or *pesa* or *hela*

month/moon *mwezi*

mother *mama*

mountain *mlima*

music *muziki*

nest *kiota*

news *habari*

nighttime *usiku*

office *ofisi*

oil *mafuta*

paint *rangi*

pants *suruali*

parents *wazazi*

path *njia*

photograph *picha*

pigeon peas *mbazi*

plate *sahani*

public bus (large) *basi la abiria*

public bus (small) *dala dala*

rain *mvua*

rice *mchele*

river *mto*

road *barabara*

rope *kamba*

salt *chumvi*

school uniforms *sari za shule*

school *shule*

season *majira*

sheep *kondoo*

shoes *viatu*

sickness *ugonjwa*

soil *udongo*

song *wimbo*

store *duka*

stream *kijito*

student *mwanafunzi*

studies *masomo*

sugar *sukari*

tea *chai*

teacher *mwalimu*

tractor *trekta*

transport *usafiri*

tree *mti*

unity *umoja*

used clothing *mitumba*

valley *bonde*

vegetables *mboga*

village *kijiji*

water *maji*

weather *hali ya hewa*

weed *magugu*

wheat *ngano*

year *mwaka*

Acknowledgments

ALTHOUGH ALL 350 STUDENTS at Awet Secondary School contributed writing to the project, the following students and faculty made up the core team:

AWET SECONDARY SCHOOL STUDENTS

Triphonia Ahho

Sylvester Aloyce

Kastuli Domisian

Fredy Joseph

Romana Julian

Heavenlight Laurent

Paul Mathew

Pius Michael

Pili Moshi

Shangwe Steve

AWET SECONDARY SCHOOL TEACHERS AND ADMINISTRATORS

Mary Baynit, *Second Headmistress*

Joseph Hotay, *English Teacher*

Herieli Malle, *Headmaster*

Pantaleo Victory Paresso,
  Geography and History Teacher

Joseph Ladislaus Twissamo,
  *Biology and Chemistry Head
  of Department*

Special thanks to the Multi-Environmental Society (MESO) Kambi ya Simba branch, whose small staff contributed to the project in countless ways. To learn more about the nonprofit What Kids Can Do and Next Generation Press, visit www.whatkidscando.org or www.nextgenerationpress.org.

What Kids Can Do, Inc.

P.O Box 603252

Providence, Rhode Island 02906

U.S.A.

Awet Secondary School

P.O. Box 215

Karatu, Tanzania

East Africa